POETRY OF LIFE VOLUME 1

Poetry of Life Volume 1

Denice Garcia Benders

HEY LOVER, MY LOVER

Hey lover, my lover—listen to what my heart has to say to you:
You say you want me and can love me; that all sounds good, but I'm
still hurting,
And I am not ready...
Hey lover, my lover—my intentions are real for you,
But my heart is still bleeding...
Hey lover, my lover—I want to have someone close to me;
I just don't have time for you to play with my heart or your games...
Hey lover, my lover—try to understand where I'm coming from;
My feelings have been so destroyed,
But most of all, mixed up in so many ways,
I wouldn't know where to begin to tell you
If I could...
Hey lover, my lover—one day you might understand, but
Today, let's try to be friends or more, but
Slow,
I need to heal first...

Victims, Victims

Victims, victims—we're looking for victims to put in our System...
Victims, victims—we're looking for victims; the cops don't like you,
The judge isn't crazy about you, so come into our system...
Victims, victims—we're looking for victims; it's getting hot out there,
And there is no money for the poor, but you keep dragging yourself into their hands,
You're giving them what they want...
Victims, victims—we're looking for victims, so if you're smart,
Get yourself together and join them;
Don't be in their system...
Victims, victims—we're looking for victims, so young mothers,
Keep your eyes on your children,
Because the system preys on them—the young and old,
And people with disabled parents,
And black, brown, and white who are less fortunate in their eyes...
Victims, victims—we're looking for victims;
Let's get ourselves together and look out for each other
For our children's safety.

Drug Kill, Lost Soul

Drug kill, lost soul—some people think this is their only way to escape
From their pain; reality is not...
Drug kill, lost soul—some people just can't handle their fear well,
But the devil gave them that faster tool...
Drug kill, lost soul—you lose everything: your children, your family, and even
Your freedom because you've been trapped in hell
That never lets you go...
Drug kill, lost soul—some people will lie to you in order to get what they want from you; it works,
But you can't see that...
Drug kill, lost soul—only because they think you're weak.
Lift up, come feel again;
See what is really going on while you're sleeping...
Drug kill, lost soul—they are not trying to hide, just creeping into your soul.
Fight them off and be strong again...
Drug kill, lost soul—stand up
And say, "I got this now,
And I'm free from this sickness I had..."
I was weak, but now I'm strong...

If I Got to Chase You, I Don't Want You

If I got to chase you, I don't want you—I notice that I am always reaching out to you,
What you can't see...
If I got to chase you, I don't want you—I notice that I'm the one who's always trying to find
Fun things for us; all you do is cancel or
Never show up...
If I got to chase you, I don't want you—here's what I notice: if you're not interested in me
Or anything that we planned, then why are you here?
Why bother me...
If I got to chase you, I don't want you—life is too short; why play this game
When you can just say what's on your mind...
If I got to chase you, I don't want you—I don't want anyone who doesn't want me
Or my time.
Just let it go...

Children of the War

Children of the war—why is this happening? Why are you so
willing to kill children,
Women for no reason...
Children of the war—isn't it because of their religion, or the color
of their skin, or eyes, or
Creed? Who are you?
You're not God...
Children of the war—we are meant to live and learn from each
other and help each other,
But that's not the case with you...
Children of the war—you wouldn't like it if someone did that to
you or your loved ones.
If you believed in love, why are you so willing to kill?
Children of the war—you slaughter those babies in half,
And kill dogs in cold blood,
And snap elderly grandparents and women
Because you feel they are useless in your eyes...
Children of the war—you sleep and have a big party,
Knowing there's a war going on.
Do you care? Hell no...
Children of the war—you promised the people you would be
Agood and strong leader for our nation,

But you lie...
Children of the war—blood is everywhere from the war you
created,
And you think you're doing something good; you're not—
It's totally the opposite.
But you can sleep so well and be proud of what you did,
Seriously...
Children of the war—we will remember your useless thinking
And your careless heart,
The deaths of those babies, children, and women
Who died in this clueless world, that you think you did so well in...

MY STRAWBERRY LOVER

My strawberry lover—that's right, I remember my friend wanted to get with you,
But you came to me...
My strawberry lover—you walked right up to me and told me your name;
Wow, you were so fine and a great dancer too...
My strawberry lover—you used to come over to my place with your friend Red,
And buy some food. We'd eat and talk, but it was so deep—talking about yourself, Even I was shocked by what you said to me...
My strawberry lover—I remember that you fed me a strawberry from your drink
And said, "Open your mouth." I felt your heat, and you looked right into my eyes.
I knew then you wanted me as I wanted you,
But why did you leave?
My strawberry lover—you took me to P-Town with a number of your friends,
But we couldn't touch each other. Did you want me then?
My strawberry lover—I wanted you so bad, but I couldn't. Why did you stop me?

My strawberry lover—you were always hugging me and kissing me,
with or without your girlfriend.
You said to me, "You've got my heart; hold on to it.
Don't let me go."
My strawberry lover—so why did you leave me
Without saying goodbye, knowing that you had strong feelings
for me?

WISH I HAD MET YOU WHEN YOU WERE SOBER

Wish I had met you when you were sober—I'm sure you could have made someone happy,
But you didn't...
Wish I had met you when you were sober—I know you would have been so much
Fun to be around...
Wish I had met you when you were sober—all the good times would have been our best times,
And all the best times would have been the great moments of our lives...
Wish I had met you when you were sober—I would never have known
If I had walked into my apartment and saw you getting ready
To take our TV out the window. I knew then you were off the wagon...
Wish I had met you when you were sober—could you have loved me then and better?
Wish I had met you when you were sober—wouldn't you have been more true to me,
Without lying to me or cheating on me?
Wish I had met you when you were sober—you would have loved being with me,

But you didn't. Instead, you stomped on me.
That's when I knew it was time to let you go...
This should be a lesson for those struggling with drugs and alcohol: please get
Help before it's too late. You're not just hurting yourself;
You're hurting your loved ones too...

You Said You Were Coming Back to Me

You said you were coming back to me—well, what happened...
You said you were coming back to me—I hear you singing to me
how much you love me.
What are you really saying?
You said you were coming back to me—I hear you went back to
your first love,
But why did you ask me to wait? Why?
You said you were coming back to me—I saw you; we spoke.
You gave me your number and said, "Call me again..."
You said you were coming back to me—I never did,
Because I remember the hurt you gave me,
But I also remember the love you showed me too...
You said you were coming back to me—I wanted to,
But I'm still hurt by you. I guess I blew that, huh?
You said you were coming back to me—all you can say is,
"I still love you,
I still want you."
Yeah, I love you too, but you hurt me badly.
I guess you were trying to come back...

STEPFATHER

Stepfather - at least, that's what you thought...
Stepfather - she wanted a father for her children, but what he really wanted...
was a role entirely different from what she expected.
What were you thinking, mama? Not me...
Stepfather - he was too busy beating and raping your child,
telling you lies, and breaking your baby's legs.
You believed him, didn't you? But what about your child?
Stepfather - setting the house on fire, leaving his child behind,
getting his flesh and blood out, telling you it's not his child. "Die,
brat!"
Stepfather - he used to beat you just because you didn't make his
sandwich right.
Was he worth it? Now what...
Stepfather - a woman's worth should be so much more powerful
than a useless man who cannot or will not love another man's child.
When you know it's time to let the dog out, keep him out...
This is for all women and men. If you're setting yourself up for a
new life,
remember who's beside you. Your children come first, before
anyone.

SINCE YOU'VE BEEN GONE

Since you've been gone—nothing has been the same...
Since you've been gone—when you laughed, the room lit up; now
it's dark and gray,
And no one is talking anymore...
Since you've been gone—everything of yours is still the same,
But you know it's gonna change soon,
Though none of us are ready for it...
Since you've been gone—some good has come out of this,
But that doesn't mean you shouldn't be a part of it.
It would be great if you were here...
Since you've been gone—our family is getting larger and larger,
And what I mean by that is one of your children
Did some research and found the other half of the family,
Oh my, you have some history to tell...
Since you've been gone—even though you have history to tell,
Who do we tell, and who is really willing to listen
About you, your life, and the beauty of the things you did
To bring others around you and us...
Since you've been gone—you told us to be strong and stand our
ground.
That's easier said than done,
But we are doing it. Are you proud of us now?

She's a Cold-Hearted Lover

She's a cold-hearted lover—yeah, that's her, but you still want her.
Now that's funny...
She's a cold-hearted lover—she's got you right by the nose,
And you're thinking she loves you?
Oh really, wake up, would you...
She's a cold-hearted lover—she tells others how she's got you
hooked.
What you gonna do, girl?
She's a cold-hearted lover—you're sitting by the phone waiting
for her,
While she's playing another girl just like you...
She's a cold-hearted lover—she's fine as wine, and she knows it.
That's why she plays the game so well...
She's a cold-hearted lover—you might wanna put her in her place
And let her know you know her games all too well...
She's a cold-hearted lover—you put all your energy into her.
What is she doing for you?
She's a cold-hearted lover—you still want her.
Ask her what she really wants; I bet she can't
Answer that with a straight face...
She's a cold-hearted lover—all she does is lie and play with many
hearts.

Oh, but you will meet your match...

My Mother Chose You for a Reason

My mother chose you for a reason—first, she wanted to say thank you
For being there for the good times and the bad...
My mother chose you for a reason—thank you, my dear friend and sister.
I never knew how lucky I was until I was sick.
You stood by me all day and night. I know I wasn't easy to deal with,
But that was because I was hurting, and I knew I would be gone soon...
My mother chose you for a reason—thank you for dealing with my children
When most of my friends couldn't grow up.
Now, if you had seen them when they were little,
I wonder how that would have worked out...
My mother chose you for a reason—now that I am gone,
I notice that you are still there for my children
And took my place in a different way as an auntie, not as a mother.
I want to thank you for that.
You might have known how I would feel about that...
My mother chose you for a reason—I chose you, Angie, for a reason.

It was God who gave me that sign, and I chose my other daughter
To get you this message because I knew she would let others know
That I am still here and I have not forgotten you.
If anything, I am so proud of each one of you,
But I am still hurting because I am not with my babies...

21

RAPE

Rape—some people cry rape, but that's not a joke. Stop playing with yourself...
Rape—it's a crime that has been around since the century. Some have been solved, and some haven't.
But what it does to you messes you up in so many ways—physically, mentally, and emotionally.
Your soul has been ripped apart, and you can't ever get it back again...
Rape—I know I've been there a thousand times in my life.
They say every ten seconds a woman or young girl gets raped at least once in her life.
That's not always true; some of us experience this all our lives...
Rape—I know I am one of them...
Rape—did anyone save me? Did anyone ask if I needed help?
Did anyone come and comfort me?
Hell no.
I held my own.
Thank you...
Rape—some of us are so messed up by the situation that we cannot tell
What is wrong or right, because some of us are destroyed.

But some of us will stand strong and will not let the creeps get the
best of them;
Others cannot handle it...
Rape—I know I am one of them...
Rape—a woman can endure as much as she can,
But if you are with her, please support her.
Never throw that in her face, making her feel it's her fault.
She will never be the same once you do that,
And best believe she will never trust you or want you by her side...
Rape—she will never forget what you did to her
And how you made her feel inside.
Everything you had is gone for good,
Because you made the wrong move...

Do You Think About Us

Do you think about us—all the good times and bad times that
we had...
Do you think about us—when the days were young, how crazy we
were together?
Do you, baby...
Do you think about us—all the crazy things we did until the days
went dark...
Do you think about us—when we drove down to North Carolina
to visit your family?
Were you thinking about us, baby...
Do you think about us—when one of your family members raped
me and put a gun
in my mouth?
Were you thinking about us, baby? Were you?
Do you think about us—were you in the room laughing while I was
yelling and crying?
Were you thinking about us then?
I doubt it...
Do you think about us—when I asked you about what happened,
you couldn't look
me in the face. Were you thinking about us, baby...

Do you think about us—when all this mess happened? Are you still thinking about us?
Don't, because you killed it...
Do you think about us—did you think I would never find out? I did, and
we are done...
Do you think about us—now don't, because we can never go back as friends and lovers...

How Deep Is Your Love

How deep is your love—funny how you came to me, telling me how you feel about me.
Is that real?
How deep is your love—why don't I see you all the time? Who are you
digging in?
How deep is your love—you were so sweet and gentle to me.
Is that for real or a show?
How deep is your love—you never told me about the other half, but you always say
you're mine, you know that, right?
How deep is your love—you always talk about our future, but why did you talk...
How deep is your love—you say let's start a family, but I pick who touches you...
How deep is your love—and you said you're mine whether I'm here or not.
You'll always be mine...

Mama Why You Kill Me

Mama, why you kill me—why do you tell others that I drowned?
I didn't drown; you put me to sleep...
Mama, why you kill me—why do you put on a fake smile and act in
court,
showing pictures of us when you didn't want me?
Mama, why you kill me—you got away from me just like you
wanted.
Are you happy, Mama?
Mama, why you kill me—you fooled the judge, the jury, and the
people
who believed in you. Can you sleep now?
Mama, why you kill me—now you are set free, dancing and
laughing
while I'm in heaven, watching every move you make.
Mama, are you happy now?

MY SUPERSTAR LADY

My superstar lady—the voice you have is slamming...
My superstar lady—you were the next Luther Vandross to me in many ways,
always coming home to sing to me day and night...
My superstar lady—so you used to say to me that you were taking cooking classes,
and you even showed me the signature from Julia Child.
You asked if I wanted to hold it,
but I said, "No, baby, that's you. You hold it..."
My superstar lady—one night you said to me,
"Baby, do you know the difference between a fucker
and making love? Come sit down next to me."
I did, with my mouth closed,
not knowing what to say. Why are you asking me this question?
My superstar lady—I asked, "Why are you asking me this now?"
My superstar lady—she said to me,
"Because I don't want to fuck you; I want to make love to you. I love you..."
My superstar lady—she said, "Let me show you what love is," and she did.
Then she asked, "Can I love two people at the same time?"
I told her, "Yes, can you?"

My superstar lady—she went to her new apartment,
told me where she was, and asked me to meet her there
and spend the night with her. But those days were gone.
Before that, she said to me, "When I'm with you, I'm your stud,
but when I'm with her, I'm her femme.
I am torn between the two of you..."
My superstar lady—on the last day you quit me,
you said, "I'm not doing this to hurt you. I love you.
Please remember that."
And then she sang to me my Luther.
My star is gone for good...

You Are a Snake

You are a snake—wow, I find out more and more shit about you
that you were hiding from me.
Okay...
You are a snake—since the time we clicked, you had plans for me.
Was it worth it...?
You are a snake—you lay in my bed, smiling in my face,
but hated me the whole time. You never said a word to me...
You are a snake—when I told you that bitch got me raped by my
cousin,
you knew all along who you probably set up with her.
But you loved me, huh...
You are a snake—you bit me so many times,
leaving me no poison, only memories. I understand now...
You are a snake—when I had my son, you came to the hospital.
What was that about?
Glad you didn't see him...
You are a snake—before that, you came to my place,
telling me to take my meds for the baby. Why did you care?
What was that all about...?
You are a snake—now it's 2023, and I just found out
that my rapist and you are living together for real,
and you are in love with her.

What the fuck was I to you...?
You are a snake—when my son was two or three years old,
you came by and asked if you could take him to the playground
because you thought I needed to rest.
Bitch, you must think I'm stupid, knowing how you feel about me
and hated me, but you'd do anything for my rapist.
So you were planning to kidnap and kill my son for my rapist,
really...?
You are a snake—I can remember you stomping on my head
because I wouldn't give you money for your hit.
But hitting me...
You are a snake—you used to come and tell me
that you had VD. I took you to the hospital.
That same bitch that you love gave it to you,
and you wondered why I wouldn't touch you.
So glad I didn't. Now, today, in 2023,
the three dogs have AIDS or not?
Did you make that up for attention?
Either way, I don't give a fuck about you now.
But I wanted to thank you for openly showing me
who you really are, and my so-called friends are,
because I see a snake who slithered her way into everybody's life
and bit them...

To Understand This

To understand this—when you tell someone how you feel about them,
what do they say...?
To understand this—when you tell that person that they meant a lot to you,
what do they say...?
To understand this—when that person doesn't respond back to you,
how do you feel...?
To understand this—when that person acts like you don't exist,
how should you feel...?
To understand this—when you're losing sleep, not eating well, and can't do the things you used to do,
how does that person feel about you...?
To understand this—you show no fear to that person who cares very little about you.
No, that's deep...
To understand this—you seem to be happy with what you did...
To understand this—can you sleep on that?
I bet you can...
To understand this—does that make you a decent and honest person?

Not in my heart, it doesn't...

When a Woman Says She Wants You

When a woman says she wants you—how do you go about that...?
When a woman says she wants you—do you take her with pride, or
do you trash her when you're done with her...?
When a woman says she wants you—do you walk up to her with a
real smile, or do you approach with a fake smile, take her phone
number, then play with her while she thinks you want her...?
When a woman says she wants you—do you call her and say nice
things to cheer her up, or are you still just playing with her...?
When a woman says she wants you—if you're not attracted to her,
or if you think you're not, say it.
Don't spray it; let her know,
so she can decide to move on or stay with you...
When a woman says she wants you—people are attracted to one
another for different reasons.
What was your reason...?
When a woman says she wants you—why let others take pictures of
that person if you're not together?
If you're not thinking about her,
then why do you call...?

You Pick the Wrong One

You pick the wrong one—oh, you thought you got a game
by playing with my heart.
You pick the wrong one—telling others that you were single, but
really you're not,
jumping into every bed you can and lying in my face.
You pick the wrong one—while you're playing dog in the heat, I'm
getting myself together.
I'm done fucking with you.
You pick the wrong one—stop barking at my door, wanting to
get in.
I'm done fucking with you; you played me that last time.
You pick the wrong one—I found your sidekick, or whatever you
want to call it.
Just keep it moving, dog. You played me for the last time.
I'm done fucking with you.
You pick the wrong one—stop telling others your sad story about
yourself.
You know that shit never happens.
I'm done fucking with you; you played the wrong one.
You pick the wrong one—you couldn't be real with me or take
me out

or be seen anywhere with you. Keep your birds; I'm done fucking
with you.
You pick the wrong one—here's what I gotta say to you:
since you wanted to play so hard and fast,
stay away from a fine chick like me with a good head on her
shoulders.
You see, I can walk with pride.
Can you? But I'm done fucking with you.

On Dangerous Ground

On dangerous ground—funny how things change so quickly in the blink of an eye, when you're not looking.
On dangerous ground—we can't go to school, work, or gyms without wearing a mask or gloves, and our lives depend on it now.
On dangerous ground—we are walking on very thin lines, and whether you know it or not, people are losing their minds being locked down.
On dangerous ground—now we are fighting for our lives, no tomorrow. Babies are dying so quickly as they come into this messed-up world.
On dangerous ground—people are trying to get into each other fast or hook up on their last lay before they die.
Now that's sad.
On dangerous ground—the LGBTQ+ community is doing the same, trying to get married, hoping they will live and die together, and they are not sure they are even right for each other.
Moving too fast and trying to catch their last breath.
Now that's scary.
On dangerous ground—they want you to vote in every right way they can, whether it's good or bad intended or cheating.
Now that's some scary shit right there.

On dangerous ground—now the food is messed up again. How are
we supposed to eat and feed our families now?
On dangerous ground—some hospitals are letting doctors and
nurses do some half-assed jobs, picking who should live and who
should die.
Now that's some deep shit.
On dangerous ground—same with policemen killing only people of
color, big or small; it doesn't matter to them.
So all this is happening to us. I'm just saying,
this shit right here,
this is the dangerous ground we're on.

My Social Butterfly

My social butterfly—you know, the one always wriggling around
and moving too fast.
Can't you just sit still?
My social butterfly—always in different beds at odd times. Do you
even know their names?
My social butterfly—but you're asking me why I won't commit
to you.
Are you serious?
My social butterfly—I can't be with someone who isn't into me
100%.
That's crazy.
My social butterfly—how many others do you tell that line to?
Can't you be serious and willing to stand by your queen no matter
what?
My social butterfly—we need love too, or should I say, I need love.

If I Was Your Girlfriend

If I was your girlfriend—would you let me call you, or would you call me?

If I was your girlfriend—would you go out on a picnic with me near the water and talk?

If I was your girlfriend—would you let me brush my hair for me and give me a warm bath for the two of us?

If I was your girlfriend—would you come to me if you had a problem, even if it's not from you? Would you talk to me?

If I was your girlfriend—would you stand by me, through thick and thin?

If I was your girlfriend—how would you treat me? Would you love me, or hate me?

Or would you be in between, pretending you're into me when really you're not? Would you tell me?

If I was your girlfriend—would you show me off with good intent or with hate?

If I was your girlfriend—how would you end our relationship? Would you do it in a wicked way?

If I was your girlfriend—if you feel that you need to be nasty and hateful toward me, keep moving.

Chemistry

Chemistry—how do you explain something so strong between two people that they are so far away?
Chemistry—I saw you pop up on my page four years ago, and now again in September 2022.
I didn't think you would notice...
Chemistry—you put it out there, saying how you feel about me in the open. Wow, really?
I didn't know you felt that way toward me...
Chemistry—you weren't shy about telling me how you feel and wondering if I was still interested in you...
Chemistry—we talked about our dreams and what we have for each other.
It was deep and heavy...
Chemistry—you said you wanted me, but how and why...
Chemistry—I want you too, but someone has to make the move...
Chemistry—but how can you want me if you're flashing your other half on social media and telling me something else?
Chemistry—but you keep saying I am yours and you're not going to let me go...
Chemistry—again, our feelings for each other are very strong, too strong to let go.

No matter who is in our lives, we still cannot leave each other alone...

You Gave Me Good Love

You gave me good love—oh wow, things have changed while I am with you. Why...
You gave me good love—it took me some time to see what I was missing...
You gave me good love—but you always twist things up and put me on the spot.
Why...
You gave me good love—it would be hard to get away from each other unless one of us decides to leave. But why...
You gave me good love—but now you're gone. What am I supposed to do now...
You gave me good love—you were very special to me in every way, but it took some time to realize that. But why...
You gave me good love—I could never misplace you with another woman, even if I wanted to...
You gave me good love—this feeling I have is real. Can't you tell...
You gave me good love—you never showed me how you truly feel about me.
I wonder what you are afraid of...
You gave me good love—but you always said I am yours and you will never find anyone like me...

You gave me good love—you know what? I think you got me hooked, but why did you leave me...

You Don't Have to Cry

You don't have to cry—in all the people in the world who really care about you...

You don't have to cry—I know you've been through hell and back, but who's really there for you...

You don't have to cry—there is someone who cares about your needs and wants and understands what you're going through. Just wait for that person...

You don't have to cry—I hope that person doesn't take your love for granted or deceive you, but is willing to stand by you...

You don't have to cry—is there a real person who's willing to help their loved one up and help them build their dream career, or are you in a hurry to break her down...

You don't have to cry—with all this hate and fake people, who can you trust...

You don't have to cry—are you with me or not? Either way, it doesn't matter. I've got this...

www.ingramcontent.com/pod-product-compliance
Lightning Source LLC
Chambersburg PA
CBHW022122150726
47990CB00003B/1467